The Attachment Theory JOURNAL

THE
Attachment
Theory
JOURNAL

Prompts and Exercises to Promote

Understanding, Increase Stability &

Build Lasing Relationships

James Nee Hundley, LCSW

**ROCKRIDGE
PRESS**

First Rockridge Press trade paperback edition 2022

Rockridge Press and the Rockridge Press logo are trademarks or registered trademarks of Callisto Media Inc. and/or its affiliates in the United States and other countries and may not be used without written permission.

For general information on our other products and services, please contact our Customer Care Department within the United States at (866) 744-2665, or outside the United States at (510) 253-0500.

Paperback ISBN: 978-1-68539-724-1

Manufactured in the United States of America

Interior and Cover Designer: Lisa Schreiber
Art Producer: Hannah Dickerson
Editor: Olivia Bartz
Production Editor: Ellina Litmanovich
Production Manager: Riley Hoffman

All illustrations used under license from Shutterstock.com
Author photo courtesy of April O'Hare Photography

10 9 8 7 6 5 4 3 2 1 0

Contents

Introduction

AS AN ATTACHMENT THERAPIST who works with individuals and relationships, I've seen the healing that understanding oneself can bring. Developing a better sense of awareness of your thinking and emotions is key to achieving more fulfilling relationships and an authentic life. Attachment theory is often associated with parent-child or romantic relationships. However, we've learned our attachment style influences relationships in every context: relationships with friends, co-workers, our community, the world, and even ourselves. Our attachment styles guide the strategies we use to get our needs met and stay safe with others.

This guided journal, designed to be a companion to *The Attachment Theory Workbook*, will enhance your journey of self-discovery and learning. It will be helpful to anyone who is wanting a better relationship with themselves and others.

You will find three primary attachment styles discussed within this journal: anxious, avoidant, and secure. A fourth style, disorganized attachment, is a result of complex childhood trauma, and those with this attachment style will not be best served through this book. This book is also not a replacement for therapy or prescribed medications. If you are experiencing debilitating depression or anxiety, please see the Resources (page 148) for help in finding support.

With the tools and insights you will gain from this book, you will find yourself closer to self-understanding. Gaining that awareness is a critical step toward bringing about the change you want to see in your life.

How to Use This Book

THIS BOOK is divided into six sections, all filled with prompts and exercises to help you reflect on how you relate with yourself and others, as well as practices to build new insights. The journal and its contents are meant to be paced so you can get the most out of the reflections and exercises. You should give yourself at least a week to go through each section.

The first section gives a general overview of the attachment styles and will help you identify your style(s). Section 2 through section 4 focus on better understanding the attachment style(s) and working toward more security in how you relate with yourself and others. The final two sections discuss how attachment styles interact with each other and how you can continue to build security in your life, even after completing your work within this journal.

Attachment styles are not set in stone. They can change with different experiences and perspectives, and they may also differ based on context. You may be secure in one relationship, anxious in another, and avoidant in others. Do not be surprised if you feel you have different attachment styles dependent on the setting. Earned security in all relationships is possible with practice, fostering self-awareness, and going to the edge of your comfort zone. This helps change your thinking and process your feelings so you can change your patterns.

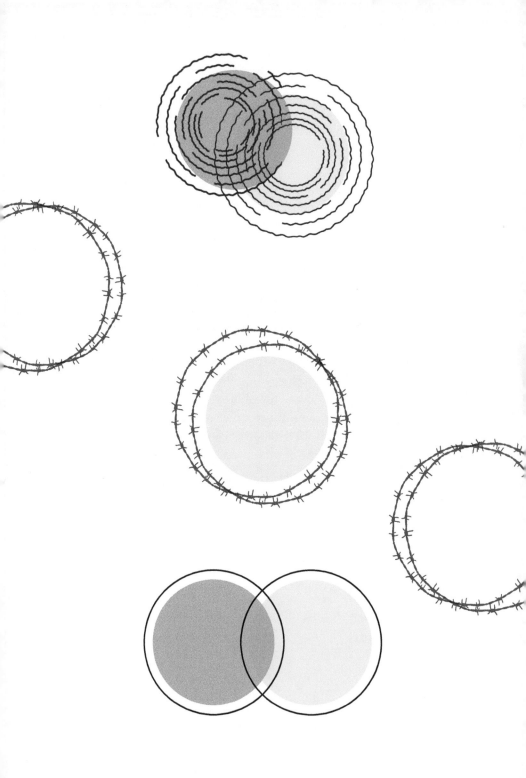

What's Your Attachment Style?

JOHN BOWLBY AND MARY AINSWORTH are the founders of attachment theory and were the first to identify the three primary attachment styles. Two of the styles are considered insecure attachments, while the third is secure attachment. Some people have a style that resonates with them across relationships, while others have different attachment styles depending on the context of the relationship.

This section will help you identify your attachment style in different kinds of relationships. The questions help identify your beliefs about yourself and your relationships, as well as what strategies you use to feel secure in a relationship when distressed.

Self-compassion drives change.
Self-judgment keeps me in place.

Relationship Attachment Styles

To learn your attachment styles, it's helpful to notice your thoughts and feelings when you think of others.

Following are common thoughts and feelings experienced by people with the three primary attachment styles.

ANXIOUS

- Afraid of abandonment and betrayal
- Often feels they need to act a certain way for people to value them

AVOIDANT

- Uncomfortable with emotions and close relationships
- Values being self-sufficient

SECURE

- Comfortable with boundaries in relationships
- Easy to honor both their emotions and the emotions of others

With these descriptions in mind, notice your thoughts and feelings during interactions in different relationships, such as with

- Authority figures
- Community
- Co-workers/peers
- Extended family
- Friends

- Parent/caregiver
- Romantic partner
- Self
- Siblings
- Society

Our experiences around receiving comfort from others influence how we comfort ourselves and view ourselves.

⚡ When you were young, who did you go to for comfort and why?

⚡ How were you received, and was it different from what you were needing in those moments?

⚡ Do you feel this impacts how you seek comfort today? If so, reflect on how.

I didn't know then what I know now.

When we were children, we did not have our adult knowledge. We hadn't had the experiences yet. Think back on yourself as a child, as a teen, and at your present age. What are three words that come to mind when you think of yourself in each stage of life?

Child: ....

Teen: ....

Present Day: ....

What themes do you notice in the words that come to mind for these phases of your life?

....

....

....

....

....

....

....

....

Attachment styles influence our relationship with ourselves. Think about your relationship with the list of common feelings. Do any images or feelings come up when you think about them? Which do you feel most or least comfortable with?

Anger: ....

....

Calm: ....

....

Fear: ....

....

Joy: ....

....

Love: ....

....

Sadness: ....

....

Shame: ....

....

To understand myself gives
me power over my life.

Attachment Insecurity Scale

Use this scale adapted from Dr. N. L. Collins's Revised Adult Attachment Scale to measure your attachment security.

Looking at the following questions, how true do these statements feel on a scale from 1 to 5, with 1 being "completely false" and 5 being "completely true"?

_____Getting close to others is uncomfortable.

_____I am nervous when anyone gets too close.

_____I am uncomfortable having others depend on me.

_____I find that others are reluctant to get as close as I would like.

_____I often worry people just tolerate me.

_____I worry about being abandoned.

_____My desire for closeness has scared people away.

_____People are not usually reliable.

_____People often want me to be closer than I feel comfortable being

_____Trusting others is difficult.

TOTAL: _____

Add your answers to reach a total score. Place a mark on the following line that best aligns with your total score to see where you fall on the scale.

10 - 50

Secure   **Insecure**

When you think of your top three closest relationships, who do you think of? What about those relationships makes them "close"?

Thoughts, emotions, and actions are all influenced by one another and are guided by our attachment style. With the following figure in mind, reflect on a time you were in conflict with someone you have a close relationship with. What thoughts and feelings do you notice? Did they guide your actions? Reflect on the same with a different conflict involving someone else. What differences and similarities do you find?

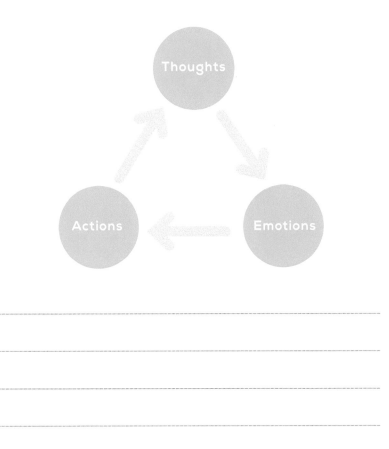

When we are distressed, we try to calm ourselves the way we were comforted by people close to us or we use strategies they modeled to us. We don't always learn healthy strategies, but self-awareness is the first step to change. How do you typically comfort yourself when you are distressed?

Relationship Quality Survey

Checking in with yourself about your satisfaction in different parts of a relationship is a healthy exercise to help keep communication going and ensure needs are being met.

Thinking of your current or most recent romantic relationship, mark the level of satisfaction in each area listed. Mark only those that apply to your situation. If you are in a polyamorous relationship, choose one of your relationships for this exercise.

Very Dissatisfied	Moderately Dissatisfied	Slightly Dissatisfied	Slightly Satisfied	Moderately Satisfied	Very Satisfied

1. Level of open communication

   ☐   ☐   ☐   ☐   ☐   ☐

2. How affection is shown

   ☐   ☐   ☐   ☐   ☐   ☐

3. Sexual intimacy (frequency, quality, etc.)

   ☐   ☐   ☐   ☐   ☐   ☐

4. How conflict is resolved

   ☐   ☐   ☐   ☐   ☐   ☐

5. How anger and disappointment are expressed

   ☐   ☐   ☐   ☐   ☐   ☐

Continued on next page

Very Dissatisfied	Moderately Dissatisfied	Slightly Dissatisfied	Slightly Satisfied	Moderately Satisfied	Very Satisfied

6. How finances are shared

☐ ☐ ☐ ☐ ☐ ☐

7. Sharing of household duties

☐ ☐ ☐ ☐ ☐ ☐

8. Level of shared interests

☐ ☐ ☐ ☐ ☐ ☐

9. Your level of respect for your partner

☐ ☐ ☐ ☐ ☐ ☐

10. Overall satisfaction with your relationship

☐ ☐ ☐ ☐ ☐ ☐

Take some time to observe the space around you. Look for two objects that represent things you would like more of in a close relationship. What are the objects, and what does each represent? Why?

Object 1 ....

....

....

Object 2 ....

....

....

When you reflect on your current relationships, do you find yourself playing a particular role? Is the role consistent across relationships, or does it change depending on the relationship?

When you think about your place in society, how do you feel about yourself? Is there anything you could do to change how you feel or view your place?

Attachment Quiz

Attachment styles are determined by a person's view of themselves and their view of others. This short quiz will help you identify your views.

Read each statement and circle either "Yes" or "No" about how you feel in most situations. Answer in general. Go with your initial thought:

1. I am allowed to make mistakes.   Yes   No

2. I believe I'm a good person.   Yes   No

3. I do not feel pressured to prove my value.   Yes   No

4. Most people have good intentions.   Yes   No

5. People can make mistakes.   Yes   No

If most of your answers are "Yes," you lean more toward a positive view of yourself and others. A majority of "No" answers mean you lean more toward a negative view of yourself and others.

Social identity theory says we seek groups of people we share something in common with. These social groups influence how we view the world and ourselves. Which of the following social identities describe you? Why or how? Feel free to add your own, in the space provided.

Age: ....

....

(Dis)Abilities: ....

....

Faith/Spirituality: ....

....

Gender: ....

....

Race and Ethnicity: ....

....

Sexual Orientation: ....

....

Socioeconomic Status and Social Class: ....

....

....

⋏⋎ Reflect on your feelings about each identity and category. How did you develop these identities? Were they assigned to you? Write about the origins of your feelings toward your identities and how they impact your present day.

After completing this first section, how are you feeling? Reflect on anything you have learned or noticed while completing this section of the journal.

_____

_____

_____

_____

_____

_____

_____

_____

_____

_____

_____

_____

Slowing Down

Our initial thoughts and feelings are important, but they do not always give the full picture. Sitting with emotions can help us better understand ourselves.

Try these steps when you're feeling stressed. This practice takes from five to ten minutes.

1. Take a slow, deep breath and close your eyes or have a soft gaze.

2. Notice thoughts and images that come up when you think about the stressor.

3. Notice the thoughts and emotions. (Are they changing? Is there a story they're telling?)

4. Resist the urge to judge or shame yourself.

5. Notice them without trying to fix them.

6. After five to ten minutes, take a deep cleansing breath, followed by slowly counting backward from 5, before opening your eyes.

Even when I don't believe it,
I deserve dignity and respect.

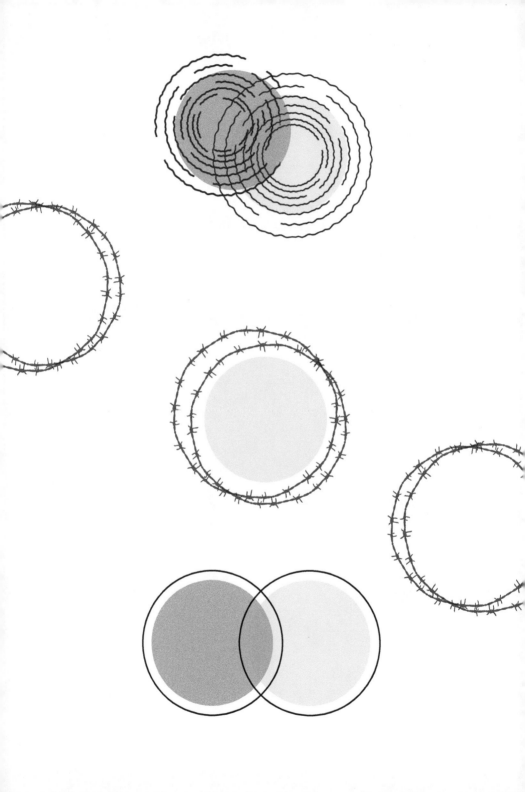

The Anxious Attachment Style

THIS SECTION is designed to help you become familiar with your anxiety and its impact on how you relate to yourself and others. Anxiety exists in all living things to provide motivation. In relationships, we are motivated to find a sense of emotional safety. Anxious attachment tends to lead us to have a low view of self but high view of others, creating the belief that vulnerability could lead to being hurt. It can also lead to mixed feelings in the relationship, because it is common to desire connection even though the relationship causes anxiety. For this reason, "ambivalence" is often associated with this attachment style.

My anxiety tells me what I fear will happen, not what will happen.

4 In, 8 Out Breath

It is important to be able to find ways to self-regulate. Having a toolbox of techniques can assist you during challenging times. One great method for self-regulation is intentional breathing.

When you feel your mind and body start to race in an anxiety spiral, try this breathing technique. Take a moment to intentionally and slowly breathe in, while counting to 4 in your head. Then slowly and intentionally breathe out, counting in your head to 8. If necessary, repeat. This technique slows your heart rate and calms your thoughts. Give it a try throughout the day, and reflect on what it was like and if it was helpful.

When you think of anxiety, what are your first thoughts? List three to five thoughts or associations you have with anxiety. Reflect on how you experience your own anxiety.

1. ....

2. ....

3. ....

4. ....

5. ....

Now that you have a sense of your anxiety, what is it like reflecting on it? Is anxiety a comfortable topic to talk about? Why or why not?

Our experiences impact our attachment style, which informs our self-narrative. This is important because our thoughts and feelings guide our actions. When you reflect on times you are anxious, what are some of the usual thoughts?

When my mind and body race, I can slow the spiral with my breath.

Generalized Anxiety Screener GAD-7

This exercise is comprised of a self-administered questionnaire that can be used as a screening and severity measurement tool for generalized anxiety disorder (GAD).

Over the last two weeks, how often have you been bothered by any of the following problems? Please circle the number that best corresponds to the frequency of experience, with 0 representing "Not at All," 1 representing "Several Days," 2 representing "Over Half the Days," and 3 representing "Nearly Every Day." When you have answered each, add up the numbers you have circled, and place the total score in the space provided.

	Not at All	Several Days	Over Half the Days	Nearly Every Day
1. Feeling nervous, anxious, or on edge	0	1	2	3
2. Not being able to stop or control worrying	0	1	2	3
3. Worrying too much about different things	0	1	2	3

Continued on next page

	Not at All	Several Days	Over Half the Days	Nearly Every Day
4. Trouble relaxing	0	1	2	3
5. Being so restless that it's hard to sit still	0	1	2	3
6. Becoming easily annoyed or irritable	0	1	2	3
7. Feeling afraid, as if something awful might happen	0	1	2	3

TOTAL SCORE: ....

(Score of 8+ indicates possible anxiety disorder.)

Developed by Drs. Robert L. Spitzer, Janet B. W. Williams, Kurt Kroenke, and colleagues, with an educational grant from Pfizer Inc. No permission required to reproduce, translate, display, or distribute, 1999.

 Positive experiences teach us just as much as negative ones. Reflect on a time you felt comfortable in a relationship. What did that person do that helped you not feel anxious about the relationship at that time? Can you recall the kinds of thoughts you had when they did those things?

When you're anxious, what are some ways you try to self-soothe? What works best for you?

We all have different relationships with our anxiety. How do you feel about yours? Do you feel comfortable talking about your anxiety with others? How do you talk about it?

_____

_____

_____

_____

_____

_____

_____

_____

_____

_____

_____

_____

_____

Helpful Anxiety

We rarely think of anxiety as helpful, but it is always trying to protect our emotional and physical safety. That's why ignoring it isn't usually effective. Taking time to be curious about what's eliciting the anxiety is a powerful tool. This strategy requires looking for the helpful intention of the anxiety so we can assess what our anxiety is wanting us to do and if it is necessary.

Think of a time you were anxious. What action did you want to take? Freezing or doing nothing is also an action. Reflect on the root of what was eliciting that response. Use the table to track your anxious thoughts and helpful actions. Once you know what the root of the anxiety was, you can address it more effectively. An example has been provided.

Anxiety- Provoking Situation	
Starting a new job	
Initial Anxious Thought	
"I made an awful first impression."	
Action(s) I Want to Do or That I Do	
Not return to work Shame myself	

What about this situation is eliciting this response?	
I want to make a good first impression. What if they dislike me and don't recognize my value?	

Helpful Anxious Thought	
If they don't like me, that isn't a reflection on my value to the employer.	

Helpful action(s)	
Keep trying my best	

Do you feel comfortable reaching out to trusted friends or relatives when you're not able to soothe your anxiety? What is it like to reach out? Is it okay for you or for others to reach out for comfort when anxious? What does it say about a person, from your perspective?

An anxious attachment creates a mistrust in ourselves and others. Reflect on what it is like when you need to trust yourself and what it is like to need to rely on others.

_____

_____

_____

_____

_____

_____

_____

_____

_____

_____

_____

_____

_____

It's common for our social identities to contribute to our attachment style depending on the identity and how that identity is viewed. Do any of your social identities contribute to your anxious attachment?

Age: ....

....

(Dis)Abilities: ....

....

Faith/Spirituality: ....

....

Gender: ....

....

Race and Ethnicity: ....

....

Sexual Orientation: ....

....

Socioeconomic Status and Social Class: ....

....

........................: ....

Body Scan

Frequent body scans help us develop awareness to ensure our anxious attachment is not fully guiding our thinking and decisions.

1. Find a comfortable position in a quiet place where you will not be interrupted for the next ten minutes.

2. Focusing on the top of your head, begin a gradual scan down your body to your feet, paying attention to physical sensations as you experience them.

3. Next, think of a time when you were anxious, and try to recall your feelings while thinking of that event. Conduct a body scan to help see how anxiety manifests in your body.

4. Use the image of the body to mark where you physically feel anxiety. There may be more than one location. Try to describe the feelings in the space provided.

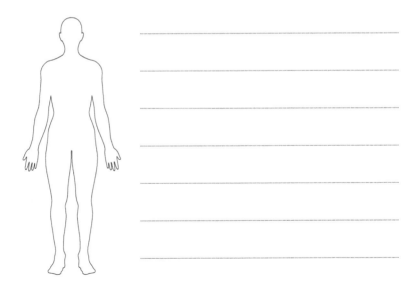

Thinking about your social identities and the ten relationship contexts, do you feel anxiety? Reflect on why or why not for each context.

Authority Figures: ....

....

Community: ....

....

Co-workers/Peers: ....

....

Extended Family: ....

....

Friendships: ....

....

Parent/Caregiver Relationship: ....

....

Romantic Relationship: ....

....

Self: ....

....

Siblings: ....

....

Society: ....

....

Reflect on what it is like to feel someone dislikes you or is disappointed in you. Describe the emotions, physical sensations, and thoughts.

Emotions: ....

....

Physical Sensations: ....

....

Thoughts: ....

....

⚡ With this information from p. 43 in mind, try identifying a helpful thought to help you tolerate the disappointment.

Once we are better able to understand our anxiety, it becomes easier to make our needs in a relationship known in a way that can be heard. Reflecting on a relationship that creates anxiety, use the skills you've gained in this section to reflect on how you can communicate your needs in this relationship.

Mindful Moment

In this fast-paced world, it's easy to get lost in the momentum of the day. This can inadvertently activate our anxious attachment defenses. Taking a moment to check in with yourself can help.

Try these steps at different moments throughout your day. You only need to set aside a minute or two throughout the day.

1. Take a slow, deep breath.

2. Notice where you feel anxiety in your body.

3. Acknowledge the anxiety without judgment.

4. Note if there is a narrative or belief driving the anxiety.

5. Validate the narrative by saying "That is a possibility."

6. Make space for other possibilities.

7. Remind yourself your anxiety alerts you to what you fear might happen, not what will happen.

Bravery cannot exist without fear.

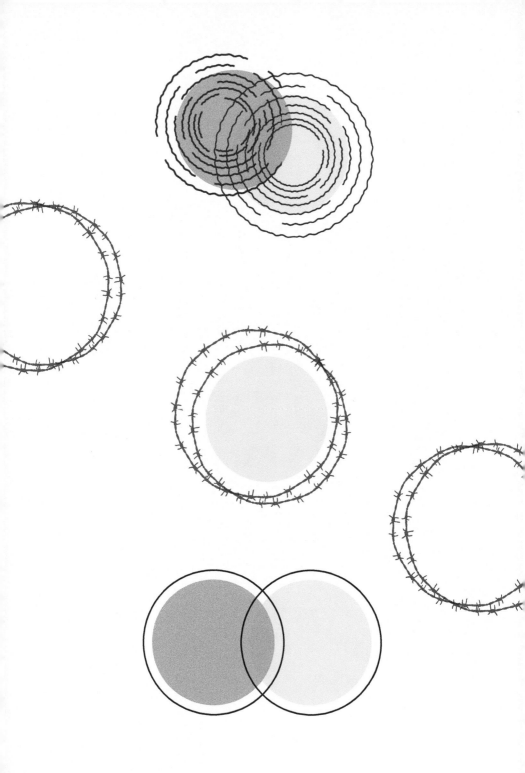

The Avoidant Attachment Style

THIS SECTION helps you become familiar with any avoidance you may have in relationships and how it impacts your relationship with yourself and others. An avoidant attachment style seeks logic and values self-reliance. You can become dismissive of the feelings and needs of anyone, including yourself. You can view emotions as irrational and as creating unnecessary conflict. Avoidance creates the illusion of safety and convinces you you're better off alone. It can suggest that people can be unpredictable, so it's safer to avoid them. The reality is that cutting off your and others' emotional needs tends to lead to feelings of isolation rather than safety.

The only constant is change—I am resilient.

Reconnecting

This attachment style creates a disconnection not only from others but also from yourself. This practice will help you reconnect with your emotions. Remember, discomfort is unpleasant, but it isn't always a bad thing. Think of it as a signal. We may want to ignore the check engine light in our car, but the car will eventually break down.

Find a space with minimal distractions where you will not be interrupted for ten minutes. Set a timer if that helps. Simply notice your thoughts, emotions, and physical sensations. Be curious about your experience. Your goal is not to change anything but to build your awareness. After the awareness is built, you can try to understand the messages you are receiving from your mind and your body. You can end the exercise by slowly counting backward from 5 and keeping a mental note of what you noticed.

Do this once a day for one week to build your self-awareness skills.

When you think about your needs in a relationship, what comes up for you at the idea of relying on others to meet those needs?

Are there people in your life you feel comfortable relying on? For many people, the context of the relationship plays a role. Consider the following relationships and list any names that come to mind. Feel free to add any observations about why it is you feel you can rely on them.

Authority Figures: ....

....

Community: ....

....

Co-workers/Peers: ....

....

Extended Family: ....

....

Friendships: ....

....

Parent/Caregiver Relationship: ....

....

Romantic Relationship: ....

....

Siblings: _____

_____

Society: _____

_____

Reflect on a time you voiced your needs with the kinds of relationships in the following list. How did those people typically respond? Can you recall the kind of thoughts you had at that time about their response?

Authority Figures: _____

_____

Community: _____

_____

Co-workers/Peers: _____

_____

Extended Family: _____

_____

Friendships: _____

_____

Parent/Caregiver Relationship: ....

....

Romantic Relationship: ....

....

Siblings: ....

....

Society: ....

....

All people need people, sometimes.

When another person is relying on you for something, what happens for you?

Checking in with yourself helps you become aware of your avoidance.

To help you check in with yourself, think of a time someone relied on you for support. Reading each statement, check off any thoughts, feelings, and physical sensations you had and actions you took.

I THINK:

- [ ] Can I provide that?
- [ ] I will fail.
- [ ] Why is this my responsibility?

I FEEL:

- [ ] Angry
- [ ] Ashamed
- [ ] Judged
- [ ] Annoyed
- [ ] Disappointed
- [ ] Overwhelmed
- [ ] Apathetic
- [ ] Guilty

IN MY BODY I FEEL:

- [ ] An increased heart rate
- [ ] Shaky
- [ ] Upset stomach
- [ ] Tension
- [ ] My jaw clenching
- [ ] Tight throat

MY ACTION:

- [ ] I become distant.
- [ ] I criticize.
- [ ] I say what I think they want to hear.
- [ ] I get quiet.
- [ ] I blame.
- [ ] I leave.

Take some time to think about how it feels to have others rely on you. Reflect on the thoughts, feelings, and physical sensations you notice to better understand any discomfort you are experiencing.

How do you go about getting your needs met? Do you do anything? Notice the thoughts and feelings you have about comforting yourself.

When you think of a self-reliant person, what three to five words do you associate with them and why? How do you know if someone is self-reliant?

My emotions are my reminder
to take care of myself.

Assessing Anger

All emotions have helpful information within them. Anger is the self-advocate of emotions. From annoyance to rage, anger is protective of you and people you care about. However, it is important to keep in mind that sometimes anger isn't the primary emotion. Once you work through the anger, you may identify a primary emotion that was driving the anger. Try this exercise to help discover the helpful intent of anger and identify if anger is the primary emotion.

1. Take a calming breath and reflect on a time you were angry.

2. Think about how you felt the anger in your body.

3. What was the anger about? There may be multiple reasons.

4. Can you identify a theme with the reason(s)?

5. With that in mind, in one sentence, what was the primary reason you were angry?

6. Does anger still feel like the primary emotion? If not, what emotion fits? Use the following list to help guide you, and feel free to add your own emotions in the spaces provided.

Anxiety   Disgust   Embarrassment   Fear   Sadness

Avoidance is a protection we develop to keep ourselves emotionally safe. With some people, we need to have walls up because they aren't reliable. Reflect on how your avoidance has helped you in your life as well as how it has not been helpful. This list will help you identify when your avoidance is being helpful and when you don't really need it.

My avoidance has helped me by: ....

....

....

....

....

....

My avoidance has been unhelpful by: ....

....

....

....

....

....

Empathy helps deepen our relationships. Empathy requires perspective taking, which is a skill we all can build. What is it like for you when you try to see the perspective of another? Describe any challenges or barriers you notice.

_____

_____

_____

_____

_____

_____

_____

_____

_____

_____

_____

⋀ Who are your three closest relationships, and what do you appreciate about them?

1. ....

....

....

....

....

2. ....

....

....

....

....

3. ....

....

....

....

....

Identifying an Avoidant Belief

Our attachment style informs our feelings and our beliefs about ourselves and others. These beliefs influence how we interpret others, how we make decisions, and how we view ourselves in the world, so it's important to practice identifying them.

Think of a time you decided it wasn't worth it to tell someone what you needed from them. Use the space provided to list all the reasons it didn't feel worth it. As you are listing, notice and write down any emotions and physical sensations that come up with each reason.

....

....

....

....

Reviewing what you wrote down, look for any similarities or themes. Themes in our thoughts and feelings help us identify beliefs. Write down the belief you identified. Is this belief helping you?

....

....

What is something you would like to change in one of your close relationships? Do you feel it's possible for that change to happen? Why or why not?

Many people are taught to be self-reliant in society and have been let down by their communities. Think about your social identities. Have any of them influenced the development of your avoidant attachment style?

Age:

(Dis)Abilities:

Faith/Spirituality:

Gender:

Race and Ethnicity:

Sexual Orientation:

Socioeconomic Status and Social Class:

Once we are better able to understand our avoidance, it becomes easier to connect with ourselves and others. This allows relationships to be more fulfilling. What insights and skills have you gained in this section, and how will you continue practicing?

Asking for Help

With this attachment style, asking for help is uncomfortable. More than likely, you've had experiences of being let down or dismissed when you've asked for help. You've learned to be self-reliant, which is a great skill, but it can cross the line to self-isolation, making you feel disconnected and unfulfilled.

Moving outside our comfort zone helps us become more comfortable interacting differently. Try asking for help from two different people and notice the experience. What thoughts and feelings came up before, during, and after asking for help?

I can trust myself to know who I can trust.

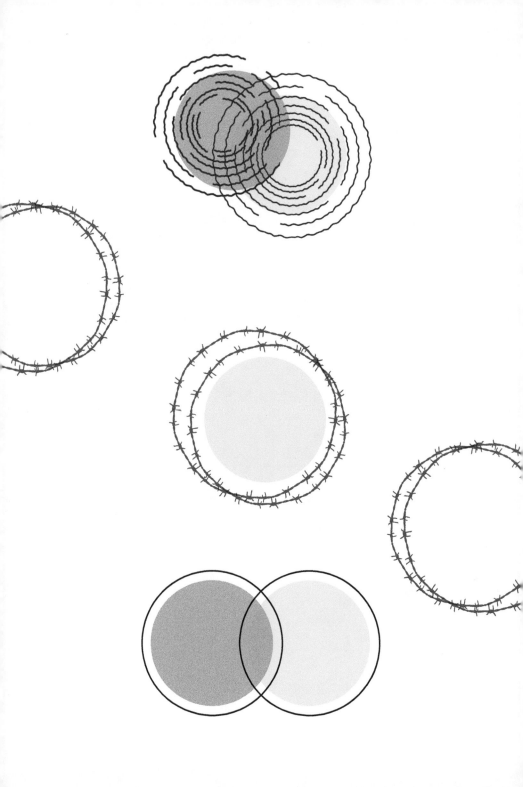

The Secure Attachment Style

THIS SECTION focuses on understanding the security you have developed with yourself and others. Even if you're still building your security, this section can help you on your journey. Remember, security can grow at any point in your life. Attachment styles are not set in stone. A secure attachment style means you can see the positive and negative in others and yourself, understanding both can exist. This is from a high view of self and others and security in who you are, making you adaptable in relationships and situations. Security allows you to be comfortable holding your boundaries with and expressing your needs to others.

I seek and strive for progress in my life.
I do not need or expect perfection.

Sharing Gratitude

We often only keep gratitude to ourselves, even the gratitude we have for others. Sharing our gratitude for other people strengthens relationships by letting that person know your appreciation.

Gratitude can be shared in many ways. You can tell someone something specific or something in general you appreciate about them. Giving a gift you made or purchased, offering an act of kindness, or spending quality time are other common methods of extending gratitude.

How are you most comfortable showing gratitude for others? Today, make a point of sharing your gratitude for a person you are in a close relationship with.

Gratitude fosters a positive mindset and helps foster security. Reflect on three things that happened today that you're grateful for.

Security is comfort in knowing that no relationship is perfect. The important thing is that the relationship is supportive and reliable. Does a specific relationship come to mind when you think of this? Reflect on what makes that relationship feel secure.

In general, how do you like to be supported in your close relationships? What does this look like for you?

_____

_____

_____

_____

_____

_____

_____

_____

_____

_____

_____

_____

My power blossoms naturally from
my true nature, not by force.

Secure Relationship Checklist

It can be difficult to know what makes a relationship "secure." All relationships look different, but there are some consistent qualities all secure relationships have.

The following list contains traits of a secure close relationship. Think of a close relationship you have and see if the relationship has these traits. Mark all that apply:

☐ Conflicts are resolved respectfully

☐ I feel listened to

☐ I feel safe

☐ It feels reciprocal

☐ It includes humility

☐ Open/respectful communication

☐ Respectful of each other, even when in conflict

☐ Spend quality time together

☐ Supportive/encouraging

A common secure belief is "I matter, and others matter." How do you remember and practice this belief?

Security in yourself gives permission to be yourself. This lessens the intensity of anxiety and creates room to acknowledge rather than dismiss emotions. Reflect on what it's like to have acceptance for your qualities that you don't always like.

Security allows us to respond rather than react. If we hurt someone we are in a close relationship with, that action does not define us, but it is our responsibility to repair it. Reflect on a time you repaired with someone you hurt. What was the experience like from beginning to end?

There are ups and downs in life, but I will pause when agitated, breathe, and move on.

Self-Esteem Level

You may be noticing security is related to self-esteem. Knowing your level of self-esteem helps you assess your level of security.

Using this scale adapted from the Rosenberg Self-Esteem Scale, rate how much you agree or disagree with each statement by circling the number that best corresponds to your response. When you're done, total up your ratings to find your self-esteem level. Scores below 7 suggest low self-esteem.

	Strongly Agree	Agree	Disagree	Strongly Disagree
I am an overall good person.	3	2	1	0
I am as capable as others.	3	2	1	0
I do not see myself as valuable.	0	1	2	3
I feel useless at times.	0	1	2	3

TOTAL SCORE: _____

Security creates confidence and gives us permission to create and hold boundaries. This can be difficult, but you can learn from your successes. Reflect on a time you held a boundary. How were you able to do that?

Like the insecure attachment styles, secure attachment also informs our relationship with our communities and our society. How did or how can you develop security in your social identities?

Age: ....

....

(Dis)Abilities: ....

....

Faith/Spirituality: ....

....

Gender: ....

....

Race and Ethnicity: ....

....

Sexual Orientation: ....

....

Socioeconomic Status and Social Class: ....

....

....

What do you need in a close relationship to feel respect? How do you show respect in your close relationships?

_____

_____

_____

_____

_____

_____

_____

_____

_____

_____

_____

_____

_____

Developing Assertive Communication

How we communicate can be a powerful tool to help us set and hold boundaries. Assertive communication is where we communicate our needs or boundaries clearly without any passivity or aggression. Reminding yourself "I matter, and others matter" can help.

Use this checklist to see if your communication is assertive.

- [ ] The emotions of everyone involved are considered, including my own.

- [ ] I'm taking responsibility for my feelings and actions, without shame.

- [ ] I am clearly explaining what I am needing without blame or aggression.

- [ ] I respectfully stick to my point if the other person dismisses or invalidates my request.

Engaging in good self-care, such as exercise, is a form of boundary because it is something we have control over. Another example is surrounding yourself with people who are respectful of you. What boundaries do you hold for yourself as self-care?

When people do not respect your boundaries or needs, how do you usually respond? Notice what it feels like and describe the accompanying thoughts. Do you notice any patterns?

Understanding security helps us develop deeper and more fulfilling relationships with others and ourselves. Reflect on what insights you have gained from this section.

The Mental Space

Our core self is made of several different traits, emotions, and defense mechanisms. These "parts" of ourselves all inform our beliefs and decisions. Use this activity to create a mental space to identify your parts and build your self-understanding.

Find a space where you won't be interrupted for ten to fifteen minutes. In your mind, envision a space that feels safe and inviting. This is your space to strengthen the relationship with yourself.

Visit this space throughout your week to get to know and understand these parts. Be curious about them and how they are trying to help you. Think how they might look, how they behave, or what they might say if you ask them why they show up in different situations.

Embracing all sides of you opens you up to being a whole person.

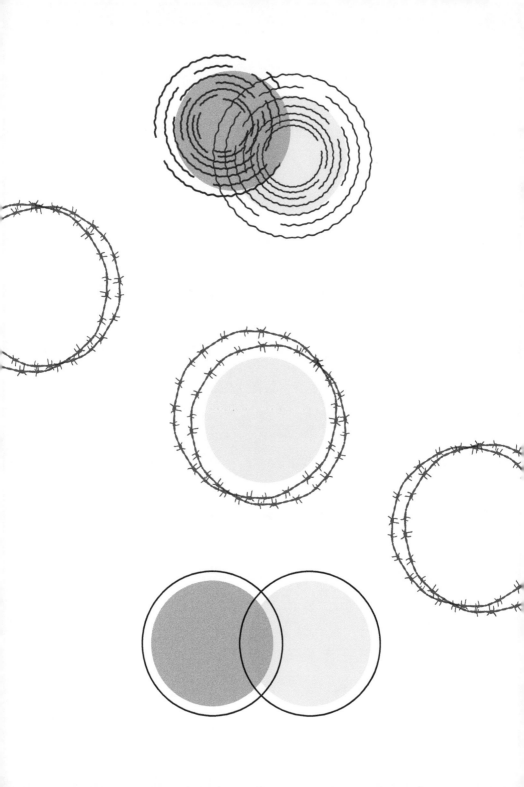

Attachment Style Interactions

NOW THAT YOU have an understanding of the different attachment styles, let's look at how they interact with each other. Like we've been discussing, your attachment style can change depending on the context of the relationship. How you know the person, how well you know them, what your experience has been with that person or people like that person, and other factors can all have an effect. Insecure attachment defenses come up when we are stressed. This section focuses on building awareness of how your attachment style interacts with the others so you can work through the stress with others with minimal conflict.

To love yourself opens you up to truly
experience love from others.

Attachment Style Interactions

Building awareness of how your attachment style interacts with others can prevent any miscommunications.

There are six major attachment style interactions. Keep these combinations in mind throughout the week and see if you notice them in your relationships.

Anxious-Anxious. Both fear abandonment, making the interaction intense where both hold little back.

Avoidant-Avoidant. Avoiding conflict, they stay on the surface level, which leads to tension and feeling distant from each other.

Anxious-Avoidant. One fears abandonment and the other values self-reliance, creating a pursuer/distancer dynamic.

Secure-Anxious. The securely attached person's comfort setting boundaries elicits the anxiously attached person's fear of abandonment.

Secure-Avoidant. The securely attached person's comfort with connection elicits the avoidant partner's dismissal and avoidance.

Secure-Secure. Both see the value in themselves and each other. When conflict arises, it is discussed respectfully.

You have done so much self-discovery in this journal so far. Take a moment to be proud of yourself for the bravery and the time you made for yourself. Reflect on what it's like to make time to notice your growth.

Reflect on a relationship that brings you joy and feels "easy." What makes the relationship so positive? Based on what you've learned about attachment styles, what attachment style do you believe this person has? This reflection helps you identify what's working and why.

_____

_____

_____

_____

_____

_____

_____

_____

_____

_____

_____

_____

_____

_____

Reflect on a relationship that stresses you out and feels like "work." What makes the relationship so stressful? What attachment style do you believe this person has? This reflection will help you understand why the two of you clash.

I cannot control the actions of others, only my response.

Understanding Our Needs

Being in a conflict can feel very disorienting. This awareness helps you better convey what you need and why it is necessary.

Think of a time you were in a conflict with someone important to you. Answer each prompt to practice understanding your emotions.

1. What behavior do you want the other person to change? ....

2. When the other person does this, what do you think? ....

3. What physical sensations do you notice in your body? ....

4. When the other person does this, what does it feel like the other person is saying to you? ....

5. How do you want to respond? ....

Saying yes or no to someone seems simple, but this can cause a lot of stress depending on the situation. Do you typically say yes or no when people ask something of you? Do you ever regret your response? Take a moment to reflect on what prevents you from being open to the other response.

Describing feelings can be difficult for many reasons. It's helpful to reflect on what happens to us when we are asked about our emotions. Do you have feelings about feelings? What thoughts, emotions, and physical sensations do you notice when you're asked how you feel or to talk about your emotions?

In relationships of any kind, we are less likely to feel insecure when we feel safe. Things like being able to joke with each other or being able to problem solve together are examples of ways we create safety. How do you create safety for others, and how do you like others to create safety for you?

Boundaries keep us together, not apart.

Attachment Patterns

Relationships create patterns based on how the attachment styles involved interact with each other. A "pattern" is made up of repeating behaviors, thoughts, and feelings that cause insecurity or security in the relationship. Understanding and untangling negative patterns is a first step in creating more positive patterns.

Reflect on a close relationship in which you've been in conflict. Describe what happens when the two of you are not getting along:

1. I let them know I'm upset by: ....

....

2. Then they usually react by: ....

....

3. Their reaction makes me feel: ....

....

4. It would be helpful to me if they: ....

....

Continued on next page

5. I think they react the way they do because: ....

_____

_____

_____

_____

_____

6. Describe your repeating negative pattern (include how you and the other person influence each other's feelings, thoughts, and behaviors): ....

_____

_____

_____

_____

_____

_____

When someone sets a boundary with you, what is your first reaction? Reflect on your thoughts, feelings, and physical sensations. How do you help yourself honor the boundary even if you dislike it?

What is it like for you when someone shares something vulnerable with you? Reflect on your first thoughts and feelings that come up. Be curious about them and why those are the initial reactions.

Listening can be a difficult skill, because we can easily get distracted with our own thoughts while someone is sharing something with us. When you're listening to someone, what are common thoughts that distract you? Are there ways you try to stay mindful of what the person is saying?

Mindful Listening

Practicing mindfulness toward others is a great way to strengthen relation-ships. However, this can be difficult for several different reasons.

Reflect on a time you struggled to fully be present when someone was talking to you. Check off any of the possible barriers to listening that seem familiar to you. Reflect on mindful practices, such as remind-ing yourself to "stay present," that can help you be a more mindful listener.

☐ I kept wondering if the person had an ulterior motive.

☐ I was preoccupied with how I was going to respond.

☐ I was trying to control the conversation.

☐ I wasn't interested in what they were talking about.

☐ Judgments about the person and/or what they were saying distracted me.

☐ Sensory stimuli distracted me (loud noises, people passing by, etc.).

☐ Something I had to get done kept preoccupying me.

☐ Other: _____

What is it like for you to share something vulnerable with someone you trust? What makes it easy or difficult for you?

In general, what relationship contexts do you feel the most comfortable in? Reflect on what makes them comfortable. How can you feel more comfortable in other contexts?

Authority Figures: ....

....

Community: ....

....

Co-workers/Peers: ....

....

Extended Family: ....

....

Friendships: ....

....

Parent/Caregiver Relationship: ....

....

Romantic Relationship: ....

....

Self: ....

....

....

....

....

Siblings: ....

....

....

....

Society: ....

....

....

....

....

The anticipation of conflict is often the worst part. When you think of being in conflict with someone, what worst-case scenarios come up for you? Do these scenarios ever end up happening?

Practice Neutral or Positive Thinking

Negative thinking leads to insecure feelings and actions. It's smart to stay emotionally safe, but if we go into a situation assuming only something negative will happen, our defenses will be up.

An example would be a friend says they want to talk, and your first thought is "They are upset with me." Your brain is going to want to analyze what this could mean. Try to stick just to the facts you have. A neutral thought would be "They want to talk with me. I'd like to know what about, and I'll find out when we meet up." That thought avoids assumptions and beliefs by acknowledging that there could be more than just negative reasons why your friend wants to talk.

Try this for a full day and notice if your interactions go more positively.

Even though some things may seem
uncertain, I can enjoy the process.

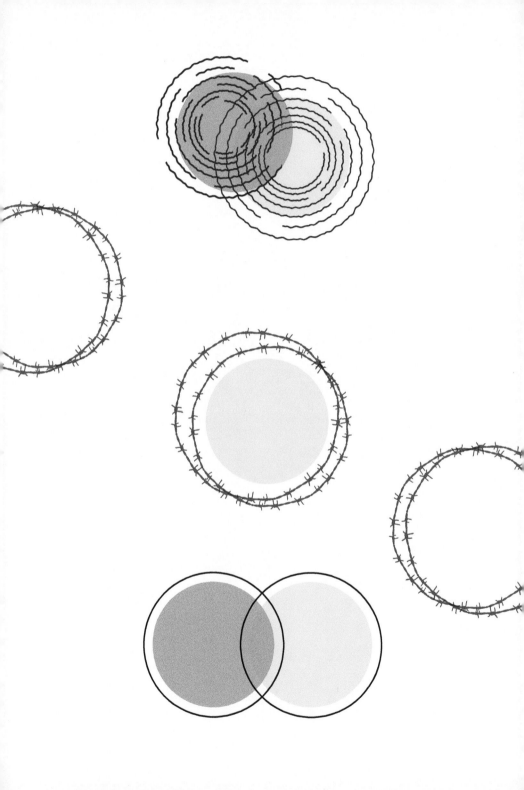

Building a Secure Future

LIVING A SECURE, balanced life is a journey. Even people who tend to be more secure in their attachment style have situations that make them anxious or avoidant. It's part of being human. Awareness and compassion can help in these situations. They're just like muscles that need to be exercised and developed regularly. After a while, they become more natural. Relationships are complicated, and even the most secure of them will have their conflicts. This section provides you with more tools to build your security. Pace yourself, love yourself, and show kindness to everyone including yourself.

I can create peace by being peaceful.

Positive Experiences

Stress activates our attachment defenses and makes us misinterpret situations. All therapies have several techniques that help us develop tools to slow down and soothe our nervous system. Focusing on a relaxing experience or memory to help us calm our attachment defenses is one of them.

Try using this practice to help you anytime you are feeling stressed or upset. Follow these steps to practice using positive experiences:

1. Think of a relaxing experience you remember well.

2. Take time to remember the positive or neutral thoughts and feelings you had then.

3. Sit with all these positive and neutral sensations for about sixty to ninety seconds. Notice what it's like to just enjoy these feelings.

4. To end, take a deep calming breath and slowly open your eyes.

Taking care of ourselves is important for building more security in our lives. We've discussed talking to ourselves in a kinder manner to care for ourselves. What are some other ways you like to recharge and take care of yourself?

Our mind and body give us signals to slow down so we don't activate our insecure attachment defenses. When you think about it, what are some signals your mind and body give to slow down? What have been barriers to listening to your signals, and how can you work with them?

Think of a person you don't get along with. Reflect on the thoughts, emotions, and physical sensations that come up and write them down. Reflect on what the experience is like.

Every day, I increase in knowledge and understanding.

Tracking Patterns

Our minds work so quickly that sometimes it's hard to know what thoughts and feelings are guiding our behavior. Tracking your thoughts and feelings is a skill to help you slow down and reflect on what happened.

Using the arrows, reflect on a time you were upset and a time you were happy. Track your thoughts and feelings that led to your action to practice. Remember, building awareness is the best step toward changing how we interact with others and ourselves.

Action of Other

Friend didn't seem interested in what I was saying.

Thought

I'm boring.

Emotion

Anxious

Physical Sensation

Like I'm falling

Action

I change the subject to them and start to shut down.

Outcome

I feel bad about myself and less likely to share things with them.

Outcome

My friend has no idea and can't correct their behavior.

Action of Other ▶ Thought ▶

_____

_____

_____

Emotion ▶ Physical Sensation ▶ Action ▶

_____

_____

_____

Outcome Outcome

_____

_____

_____

When someone hurts your feelings, what is your first reaction? Noticing that, take a deep breath and reflect on what you are needing from the other person. How can you go about asking for that?

When someone tries to repair with you after they've hurt you, how do you typically receive it? Without judgment, reflect on your initial thoughts and feelings and why they came up.

It's rare that people have purely negative intentions toward others. People usually have neutral or well-meaning intentions. Use the following space to reflect on a person who is currently bothering you. Notice the negative intent your mind is assuming that person has and try to think of two or three possible positive or neutral intentions that person may have.

There are no failures, only
lessons, and I love to learn.

Positive/Neutral Thinking

We are good at noticing our shortcomings and things we dislike about ourselves. This can cause "blinders" that put us in a negative mindset and activate our insecure attachment defenses. To help have a more balanced view, we want to work on a neutral or positive mindset.

To build this skill, list five positive or neutral words that you feel describe yourself:

1. ....

2. ....

3. ....

4. ....

5. ....

Reflecting on each word, note any initial thoughts, emotions, or physical sensations that come up when you think of each word. Approach each with curiosity and reflect on why each word elicits the thoughts and feelings.

....

....

....

....

⚡ Reflect on at least two times you experienced success. Note how you think about yourself and what self-talk is there for those situations. Are you able to feel the success, or do you minimize it? What is it like to celebrate your accomplishments? If it's difficult, be curious about that.

⚡ Think of a time you were embarrassed or made a mistake in front of another person. Reflect on the thoughts, emotions, and physical sensations that come up and write them down. Think of some helpful phrases you can encourage yourself with.

What are strengths or positive qualities other people have used to describe you? What is it like for you to receive positive feedback from others? Be curious about why that is.

The Mediation Room

Everyone has experienced internal conflict. Part of you thinks something is a good idea but another part is unsure. This exercise can help.

Find a calm space where you won't be interrupted for fifteen to twenty minutes. Take a deep breath and envision what you would like your mediation room to look like. This is your space to problem solve.

Thinking of an internal conflict you have, read the prompt and write down what you notice.

List out what each part wants you to do. Most likely, both parts will have good points.

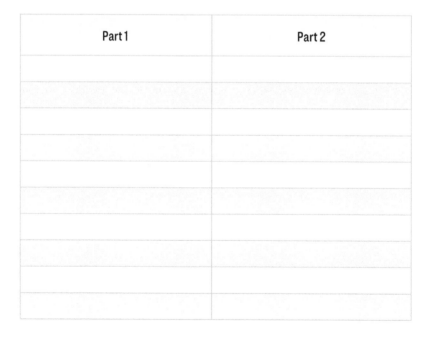

Part 1	Part 2

Using this space regularly will help you make decisions and build stronger self-awareness.

Keeping your social identities in mind, write at least two strengths you find in each identity.

Age: ....

....

(Dis)Abilities: ....

....

Faith/Spirituality: ....

....

Gender: ....

....

Race and Ethnicity: ....

....

Sexual Orientation: ....

....

Socioeconomic Status and Social Class: ....

....

....

It's normal to look back at our past selves and feel upset with our past actions or points of view. You didn't know then what you know now. Reflect on your past self and write down specific things you either forgive your past self for or are working on forgiving your past self for.

⩗ What are two or three things you will practice each day to continue building a secure future for yourself, and how will you stick to them?

Run the Simulation

A way to navigate stressful interactions is to envision our future selves in them. Our brains prepare us by running mental simulations where we can imagine how we might be thinking and feeling in the future.

Think of a specific interaction coming up soon that is stressing you out. Start from the beginning and run through what you think it will be like, noticing details as you go. Now reflect on the following prompts to decide how to best handle the situation.

Imagine the following:

- How can you respond, rather than react?

- How can you encourage yourself to think more neutrally?

- How can you manage your emotions?

- How can you relax your body if it's tense?

- What are your thoughts?

- What emotions and physical sensations are you feeling?

My past is not my prophecy.
I create who I become.

Continuing Your Journey

TAKE A MOMENT to feel pride in yourself and the bravery you've shown! These were not easy questions to reflect on, but you've taken the time and expended the energy to gain new skills and perspectives about yourself and others that will help you in every aspect of your life. Building a secure attachment is a lifelong journey that involves compassion for yourself and others, slowing down, and awareness. This is just one step to better understanding attachment theory and yourself.

Revisit the practices and exercises in this book often to see if your answers and perspectives change as your journey continues. Take a moment to look at the Resources (page 148) and the References (page 150) so you can continue learning about attachment to further develop security in your relationship with yourself and others.

Pace yourself as you continue to better understand yourself and others. You'll have days where you feel grounded and connected and days where you'll feel insecure and uncertain. This is part of the human experience. However, as you develop more security within yourself, you'll find the good days will be more common.

Resources

Books

Hold Me Tight by Sue Johnson: This book is informed by attachment science and current research. Dr. Johnson has helped many people in romantic relationships forge better connections.

Polysecure by Jessica Fern: Dr. Fern writes about the most current attachment science in her latest book.

Podcast

Attachment Theory in Action: This is an informative podcast hosted by attachment therapist Karen Doyle Buckwalter where she discusses attachment theory with other experts in the field.

Websites

EMDRIA.org: This website is a helpful resource to learn more about EMDR therapy, trauma, and attachment as well as find a certified EMDR therapist.

EstherPerel.com: This is the website for Esther Perel, an accomplished relationship and sex therapist who stays current on attachment science.

Gottman.com: This website features articles, blogs, and much more about attachment and the research the Gottman Institute has contributed to attachment science.

ICEEFT.com: This website is a great resource to learn more about attachment style interactions and to find a relationship therapist certified in Emotionally Focused Therapy (EFT).

LGBTQandAll.com: This website is a resource where you can learn specifically about mental health and attachment as they pertain to the LGBTQ community.

PsychologyToday.com: Filled with articles related to attachment and all other fields of psychology, this resource is extremely valuable. It also has a therapist finder tool.

References

Ainsworth, Mary S. 1989. "Attachments beyond Infancy." *American Psychologist* 44 (4): 709–16. doi.org/10.1037//0003-066x.44.4.709.

Beck, Judith S. 2021. *Cognitive Behavior Therapy: Basics and Beyond.* 3rd ed. New York: The Guilford Press.

Collins, N. L. 1996. "Working Models of Attachment: Implications for Explanation, Emotion, and Behavior." *Journal of Personality and Social Psychology* 71 (4): 810–32. doi.org/10.1037/0022-3514 .71.4.810.

Fern, Jessica. 2020. *Polysecure: Attachment, Trauma and Consensual Nonmonogamy.* Portland, OR: Thorntree Press.

Forgash, Carol, and James Knipe. 2012. "Integrating EMDR and Ego State Treatment for Clients with Trauma Disorders." *Journal of EMDR Practice and Research* 6 (3): 120–28. doi.org/10.1891 /1933-3196.6.3.120.

Gottman, John M., and Nan Silver. 2018. *The Seven Principles for Making Marriage Work.* London: Seven Dials.

Gray-Little, Bernadette, Valerie S. L. Williams, and Timothy D. Hancock. 1997. "An Item Response Theory Analysis of the Rosenberg Self-Esteem Scale." *Personality and Social Psychology Bulletin* 23 (5): 443–51. doi.org/10.1177/0146167297235001.

Hogg, Michael. 2016. "Social Identity Theory." In *Understanding Peace and Conflict through Social Identity Theory: Contemporary Global Perspectives*, edited by Shelley McKeown, Reeshma Haji, and Neil Ferguson, 3–17. Switzerland: Springer International Publishing.

Johnson, Susan M. 2019. *Attachment Theory in Practice: Emotionally Focused Therapy (EFT) with Individuals, Couples, and Families.* New York: The Guilford Press.

Kiessling, Roy. 2005. "Integrating Resource Development Strategies into Your EMDR Practice." In *EMDR Solutions: Pathways to Healing,* edited by Robin Shapiro, 57–87. New York: W. W. Norton & Company.

Linehan, Marsha M. 2015. *DBT Skills Training Handouts and Worksheets.* 2nd ed. New York: The Guilford Press.

Parnell, Laurel. 2013. *Attachment-Focused EMDR: Healing Relational Trauma.* New York: W. W. Norton & Company.

Shapiro, Francine. 2018. *Eye Movement Desensitization and Reprocessing (EMDR) Therapy: Basic Principles, Protocols, and Procedures.* 3rd ed. New York: The Guilford Press.

Spitzer, Robert L., Kurt. Kroenke, Janet B. W. Williams, and Bernd Löwe. 2006. "A Brief Measure for Assessing Generalized Anxiety Disorder: The GAD-7." *Archives of Internal Medicine* 166 (10): 1092–97. doi.org/10.1001/archinte.166.10.1092.

Waters, Everett, Judith Crowell, Melanie Elliott, David Corcoran, and Dominique Treboux. 2002. "Bowlby's Secure Base Theory and the Social/Personality Psychology of Attachment Styles: Work(s) in Progress." *Attachment & Human Development* 4 (2): 230–42. doi.org/10.1080/14616730210154216.

Acknowledgments

I WOULD LIKE TO TAKE A MOMENT to thank my friends, family, and husband for all the support and encouragement they have given me through my career. I would also like to thank my mentors, Dr. Robert Allan and Dr. Elizabeth Legg, for their time and guidance as I continue to develop as an attachment and trauma therapist. I have learned so much from you both! I dedicate this book to my grandfather, Bill Jordan, who started me on my path to make the world a more loving place and see the value in myself and others.

About the Author

 JAMES NEE HUNDLEY is a licensed clinical social worker in private practice and an adjunct instructor for the University of Denver's Graduate School of Social Work. James specializes in attachment and trauma using a therapeutic approach incorporating evidence-based practices and current neuro- and attachment science to help his clients get in touch with every aspect of themselves, building self-awareness to create compassion and motivate healing and change. James primarily practices emotionally focused therapy (EFT) to help relationships and families better connect. A certified eye movement, desensitization, and reprocessing (EMDR) therapist, James uses this modality to help his clients heal from all forms of trauma.